The Seesaw Missile Launcher
and Other Parenting Fails

The Chuckle Every Parent Needs!

Written and illustrated by John David Kegg

This story is dedicated to my siblings, Laura and Tom, for…well…you know.

Disclaimer: The characters in this book are entirely fictional. Big time. Any resemblance to actual persons, living or dead, is completely coincidental. Seriously, I cannot imagine anyone wanting to admit to resembling even a tiny bit anything in this book, but I suppose some people believe everything is about them. It's not. It's fiction. Really silly fiction written after the trauma of raising my children.

Copyright 2023 by John David Kegg. All rights reserved, including the right of reproduction in whole or in part in any form.
ISBN: 979-8-9892095-2-1

Introduction - Right Under Our Noses

Four time survivors of raising kids, once my wife and I figured out where they were coming from, we put a stop to THAT nonsense. I truly believe there should be participation ribbons for every parent, albeit likely splattered with stains from the ever-present urine, crap, and vomit that haunt us to this day. We earned them. Then again, such decorations would have admittedly looked like camouflage in our house.

All the parenting books and videos and advice in the world failed to prepare us for raising our children. In fact, raising is a strong term. I liken child rearing to corralling cats. Feral cats. Bad smelling, feral cats.

The one thing that I can guarantee any parent is that they are going to need to laugh on a regular basis. That is why this book exists. So, please feel free to have a chuckle at our expense. I will neither admit nor deny that some of these stories actually happened to me and/or those entrusted to my care. And to be clear, all four of my kids are now young, thriving adults - I can only assume because of the influence of their mother.

"We raised them to know wrong from right.
Stand tall, but never pick a fight.
Value learning, show respect,
be patient and be circumspect.
Help the fallen, one and all.
Be the rise before the fall.
And yet despite our wisdom sage,
somber passed from age to age,
we seemed to be a little lax -
a couple things fell through the cracks."

JDK

Flaunted, Haunted

The boldest of all, my brazenest child.
My trash talking kidder, straight out of the wild.

She dared me to take her to a charity scare.
Though eight years of age, she was sure how she'd fare.
So we waited in line while she bantered with ghouls.
With her rapier wit, made them look all like fools.

Then it was our turn; we entered the house.
As the door clicked behind, with the whisper of mouse,
she uttered some words, and I'm not so sure how.
All she said to me was, "I want out of here…now."
But the man at the gate quoted fireman code.
We had to move forward to leave the abode.

When a ghoul came a walking,
she froze on the spot.
Her eyes became glazed
and she flushed as if hot.
She could not be moved.
Her legs would not bend.
So I fireman hauled her.
No help from her end.

I trudged through the first floor,
and then up the stairs.
The monsters looked worried.
I think they were scared.
Then down flights of stairs to the basement and out,
through the back door while huffing and puffing about.
As they gave me some oxygen, monsters confessed.
'Twas the largest spook house in the whole damn US.

The Mixed Blessing

Enormous tube of A+D,
a blister busting ointment be.

Yet, left alone, my toddler ate
four solid fistfuls - sealed his
fate.

To Poison Control the call
was made.
In dire straights, we feared
we strayed.

The dispatcher couldn't help
but laugh,
while sharing news from the
medical staff.

No need to wring our hands
that day.
"Pure Caster Oil," was all
she'd say.

So we sit and wait for hours
now - our prayers still fill the
halls.
As our kid continues pooping,
fecal finger painting walls.

The Monster Beneath Your Bed

Crammed beneath my child's bed, no plan per se in mind.
Bored and waiting, wedged in place, as ticking passes time.

Now little stomping feet on stairs, approaching Daddy's hidden lair.
The bed is pressed upon my chest, an ode to cardiac arrest.

My child jumps repeatedly, then settles down to play.
And though I hear a cracking rib, determined do I stay.

I grab the frame and slowly lift - the noise above me ceases.
My little soldier searches for what's hidden in the creases.

She slowly tugs the bedskirt up to see what she can find.
A banshee shriek of *"Gobble Gobble!"* is all that comes to mind.

She's doing so much better now. No longer wets the bed.
The therapists say her nervous twitch has all but finally fled.

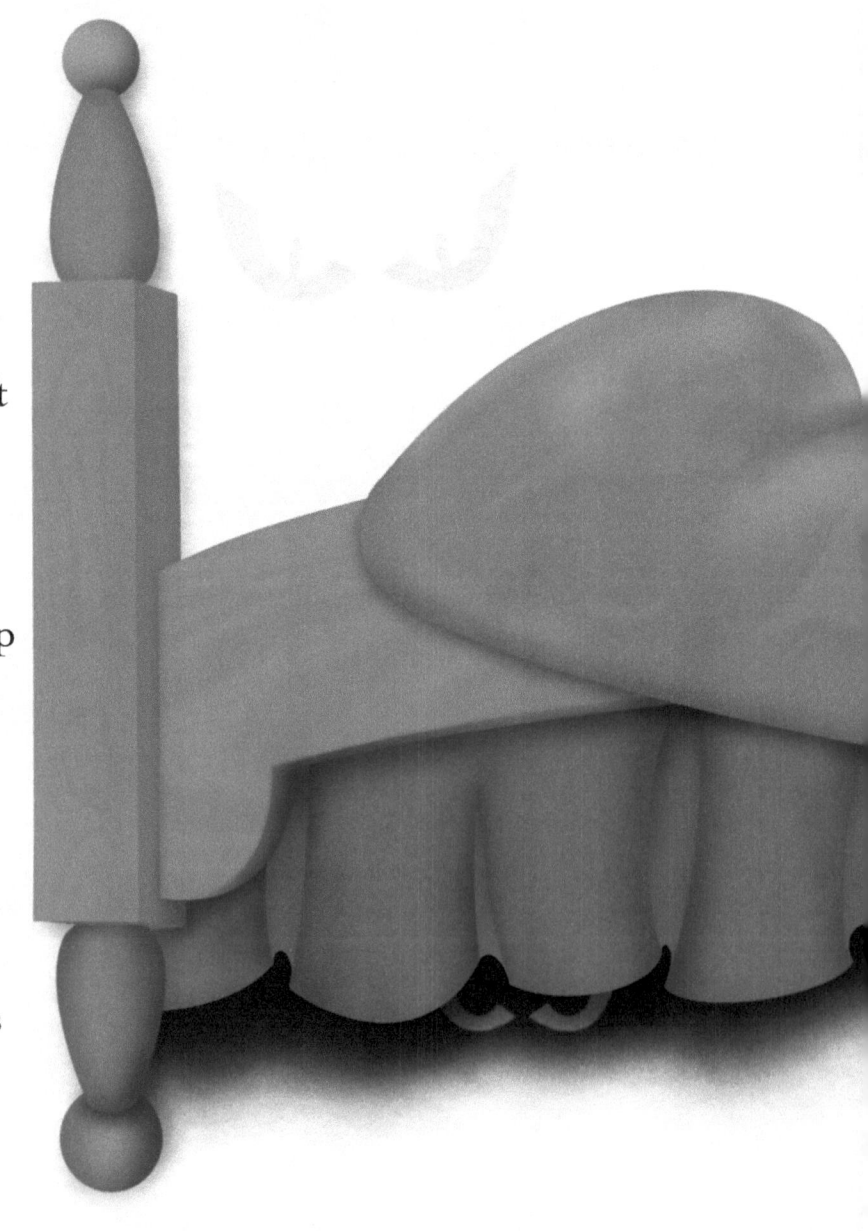

The Seesaw Missile Launcher

Nothing like a seesaw that can turn back hands of time.
The workhorse of the playground with the rhythm of a rhyme.

Always one kid sailing up while one is sailing down,
with the balance of the fulcrum that makes smiles out of frowns.

And yet I'm fairly certain it escaped the engineers
to consider *my* four children as they tinkered with the gears.

I saw them launch my youngest nearly halfway 'cross the yard.
Their combined weight on the other side, in hopes that he'd be scarred.

A seesaw at the curbside now - the eve of Garbage Day,
with all four kids strapped to it…and a sign to "Haul Away".

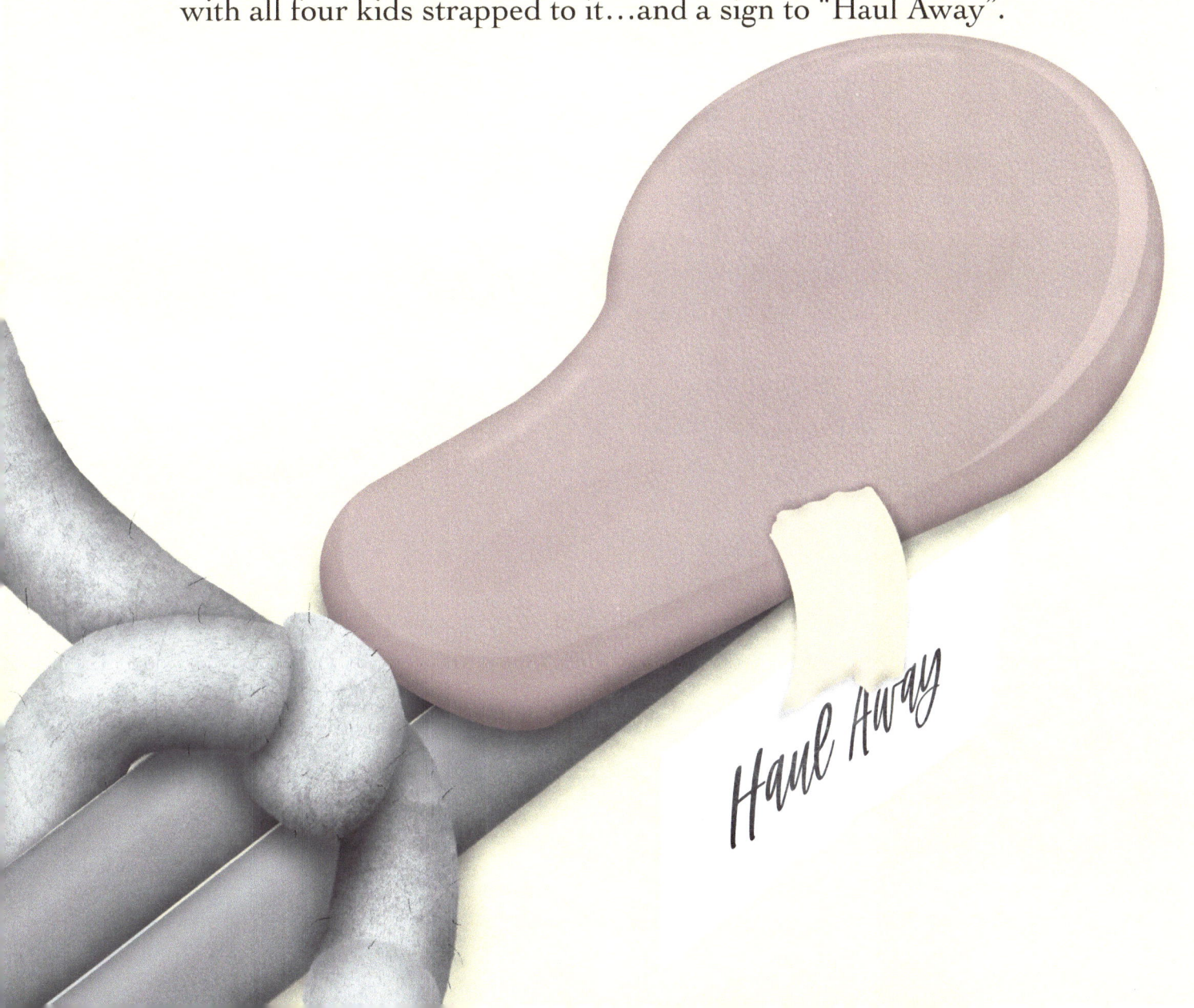

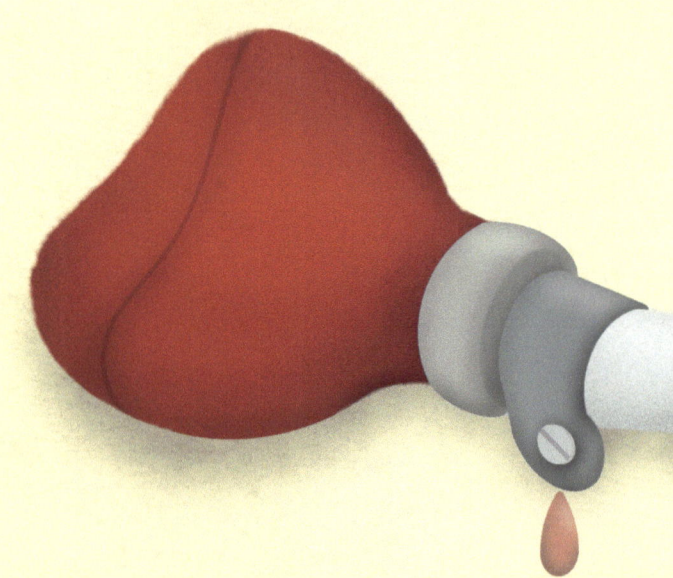

Way-to-Go Will

Way-to-Go Will, always up for a thrill.
The danger-est daredevil, king of the hill.

He probably shouldn't have taken the dare - a warning to the wise.
To barrel down a slippery slope on a bike one third his size.

No brake pads to speak of,
the chain was too loose.
The handlebar horn sadly
sounds like a goose.

With tassels, and rust flakes,
and a gold speckled seat…
…like a molded banana - the image complete.

But there he was, screaming, doing near forty-five
as he launched past the handles in a brave, graceless dive.

I guess he is grateful his heart is still beating.
A lesson was learned that a life can be fleeting.

Now he's pumped full pain meds two months in his bed
with a bicycle horn that's still stuck in his head.

Plink and Clink

Any kid knows that you always deny
when you swallow some objects - you just gotta lie.

Or forever you'll wear heavy shackles of shame,
the dopiest 'dunce' in a cap with that name.

So the jury is out at least one to two days,
as you sweat sphincter bullets, your colon ablaze.

You've hydrated well and you hope for the plink
that is followed by the telltale porcelain clink.

Yet you wonder aloud if the process is shorter
when swallowing dimes… instead of a quarter.

Give Him a Hand

The traveling minstrel puppet shows were once a thing sublime. Now mannequins and hand puppets fill landfills lost to time.

My friends still whisper stories of the toys they had as kids, those always staring blankly with their never blinking lids.

Just sitting in the corner of a bedroom every night, their soulless eyes accusing in the pale moon of light.

But puppets never bothered me; I never spared a thought, despite their cold demeanor and the creepy tales fraught.

Admittedly, for me, the case is one I quickly shut. I just can't take them seriously - a hand is up their butt.

Cones 'n Groans

My head against the dashboard, in vain hope the bag deploys.
I'm pulling double duty parallel parking with twin boys.
My brow is beading nervous sweat - I simply can't contrive…
how the Hell one hit five cones before he put the car in 'Drive'.

Fire Hose Harry

He came to be known as Fire Hose Harry.
When it came to his bladder, he just couldn't tarry.

He never met porcelain he didn't like,
a magnetic attraction since he was a tike.

Bad luck dealt a blow when he got in some trouble.
He was stuck in his room till he almost saw double.

But his mother had told him he needed to stay
till her anger with Harry had faded away.

Well, from that moment forth when the heat would come on,
our eyes would start tearing and breath burned when drawn.

The stinkiest stink would creep all through the home.
The urinal kind that seeps into your bones.

Weeks and weeks passed, yet the household still smelled.
We searched every room - the eighth level of Hell.

When beneath the interrogators light,
Fire Hose broke, gave us all quite the fright.

Harry admitted that when he went,
he peed inside the heater vent.

Which quickly through the pipes did dart,
now forever in our lungs and hearts.

A lesson was learned on that darkest of days
about the tiniest bladders one can't hold at bay.

When doling out punishments to your young pup,
just leave a large bottle when you lock the kid up.

Crafty Carver

Quite the little carver
did my sister yearn to be.
And yet when it was time
for blame,
she'd always point at me.

The dining table.
A big shade tree.
The neighbor's cat.
Each carved with glee.

The station wagon.
A passing crane.
Her brand of art
displayed her name.

I did my best to tell them
where blame should
really fall.
A loss for words betrayed
me as an infant two feet
tall.

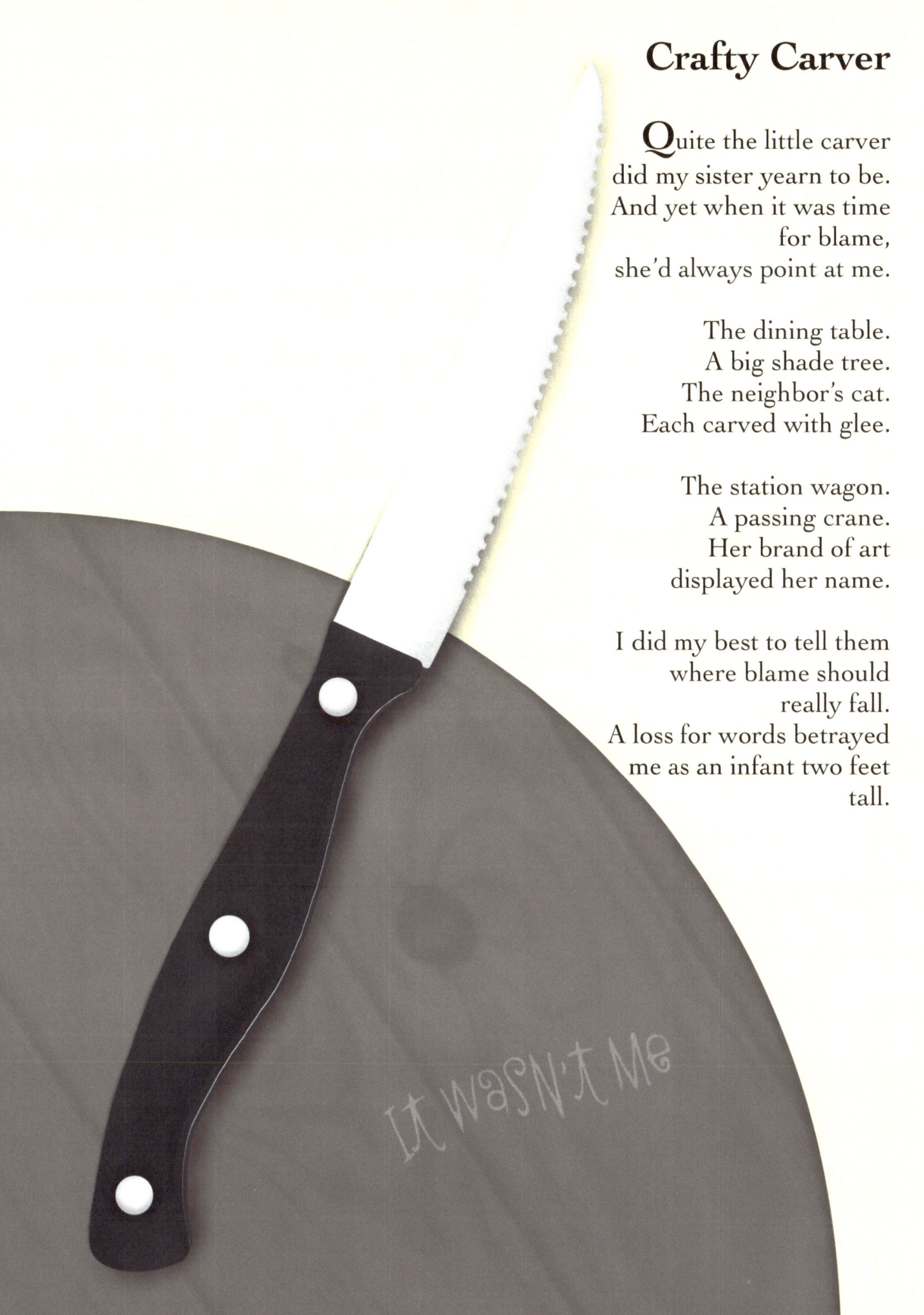

Tapestry of Words

I've always had a knack for weaving tapestries of words,
deftly leveraging four letters in a masterpiece of slurs.

Some say the surly sailors are the ones who weave the best.
Others claim construction crews could put that to the test.

But no one can quite match the skills – no color, race, or creed…
My darling little daughter caused her teacher's ears to bleed.

Ground Fault George

Ground Fault George planned a shocking
show for the science world that day.
He was a mini PT Barnum who had made
our hair go gray.

He pried the cap from a wall outlet in only
seconds flat,
to prove if curiosity could really kill the
cat.

But the cat had just nine lives
and it's fur still prickled with hives
from the first eight tests in amp and volt,
as George prepared for a final jolt.

Parking Parker

We somehow raised a Parking Parker.
Smooth talkin', struttin', teenage barker.

Six feet tall, one twenty three.
Geek to the core, we just can't see…
the attraction as they come around.
In Parker's backseat they'll be found.

Rumor has it from his mom
they've boycott Parker at senior prom.

The Talk

We had the 'talk' as parents should,
and did for children what we could.

Of birds and bees and whatnot, shared with honesty and heart.
To set the record straight and tear the sacred myths apart.

We didn't mention praying mantis biting off mates heads
or famed black widow spiders who would feed upon the dead.

While debunking all the whispers touting cabbage patch and stork,
it was sperm and eggs and pie charts told with simple words for dorks.

We kept it scientific - contraception, birth control.
Yet champions of abstinence and faith and heart and soul.

There may have been an overkill on mangling disease
and an emphasis on dead end jobs supporting pregnancies.

And maybe not enough of being smitten and in love,
an attempt to be pragmatic vs. hormone push and shove.

A little overzealous as we played the parent part.
A tiny bit protective, but it came right from the heart.

Our kids just roll their eyes and snort and slowly shake their heads,
the demeanor of a zombie found amongst the walking dead.

For we're surrounded by a grandkid throng in smirking twist of fate,
watching *Cheaper by the Dozen* 'cause we talked to them too late.

Little Brother

Little brother had a favorite park.
He'd play for hours 'til almost dark.

While Dad and others played games of catch,
or a dueled a grueling tennis match.

Then back to home we'd go,
exhausted head to toe.

And pull into the drive.
So drained, but so alive.

Mom waiting at the door,
always ready to implore…

"Where was our little brother?"
with the coolness of a mother.

And out the door my dad would fly
to quickly find my brother, sly.

Curled in a gentle ball,
rocking back and forth and all.

This may have happened once or thrice.
He took it all in stride, suffice.

We do not ask him why or how
he lives inside a large box now.

In the corner of a little park,
with his memories of the after dark.

Dapper Dan

We used to have a Dapper Dan,
to teach our sons to be a man.
Of buckles, zippers, buttons, and strings,
he taught them oh so many things.
But of dating, he was circumspect;
Dan's man parts just weren't sewed
correct.

Finger Painter

I raised a little finger painter,
decorating walls.

Didn't matter if the kitchen
or the bathroom or the halls.

He painted in three colors - yellow,
pale green, and rose.

From his little painting palette that he
kept inside his nose.

The Weird Kid

Always was the weird kid – never really did fit in.
Bright and so creative, with the pasty, blotchy skin.

Wears the bottle glasses and the nose protector too.
Always doing things the other normal kids don't do.

Reading when not studying, just loves to take a test.
Striving for perfection with the goal to be the best.

Orchestrating music when not copyrighting plays.
Loves to dance the ballet, painting masterpiece by day.

Doesn't drink, doesn't smoke, doesn't want to boogey down.
Just avoids the social aspects of a kid about the town.

I know I should feel grateful, and sometimes I really do.
But why is it too much to ask for a normal child too?

Big Wheel in the Sky

Nothing quite contains
the chilling awesomeness
and thrill
of the 20 pounds of
plastic as it hurdles down
a hill.

The tread upon the
wheels has long worn
away with time.
The colors have all faded
from the sun and wind
and grime.

Wind whispers in my ears
the Big Wheel tales of a
bard
and it begs me pull the
hand brake while I jerk
the steering hard.

At 20 mph, the black mag
wheels leave the ground.
I feel it in my nut sack
where my steel nerve is
found.

Low and near invisible, I
whip between parked
cars.
The best damn Christmas
present that I got from
Dad by far.

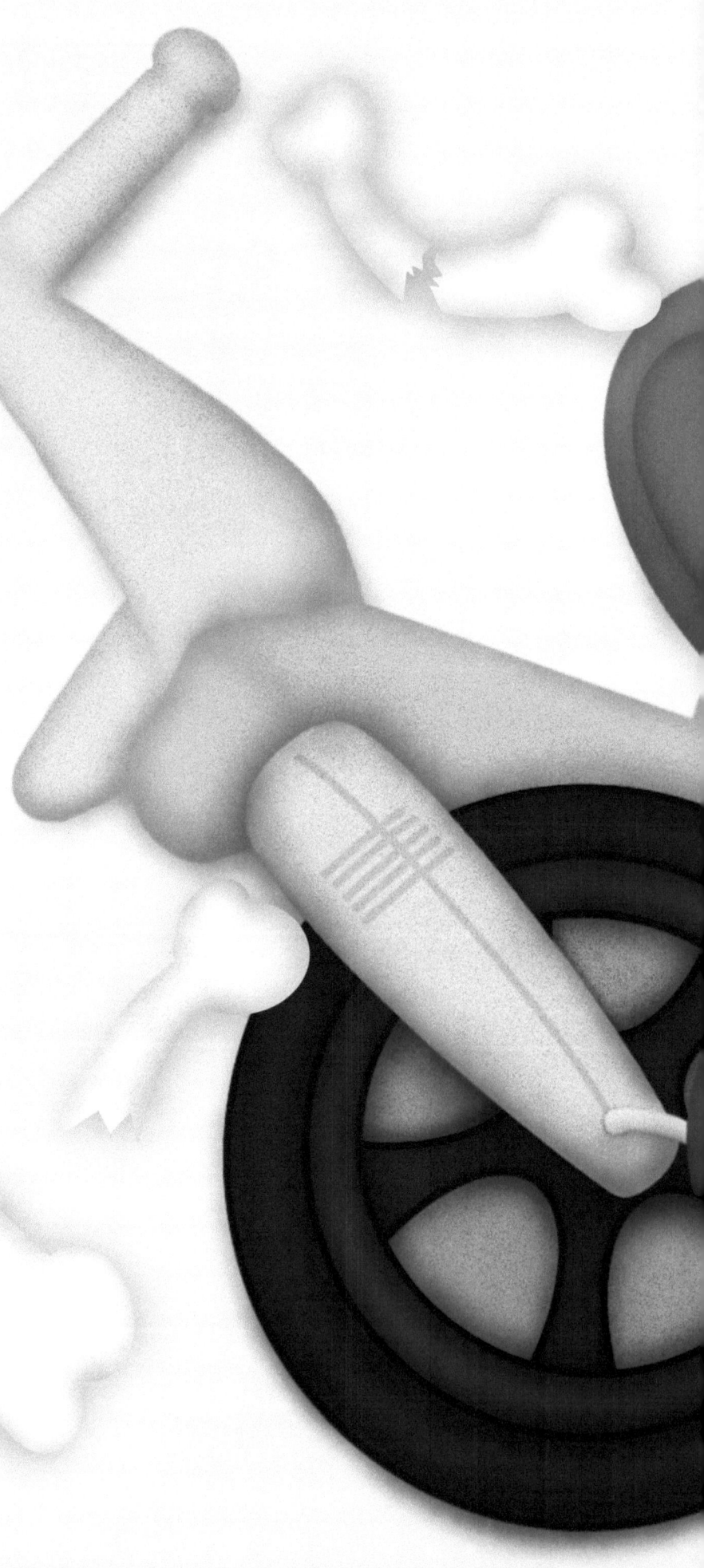

Trench Coat Toby

Toby shows up night or day.
We know to never ask…

What truck his wares are falling from.
He never fails the task.

Just text a simple photo,
a time, and private place.

He'll show up in his trench coat,
as his collar hides his face.

And in his many pockets,
all our whispered secrets hide.

The perfect match for wayward pets.
In him, you can confide.

He's Darwin's little helper and he doesn't really care
if you vacuumed Stuart Little
who you squashed beneath a chair.

Rosy Nosy

We sit here in amazement in the doctor's waiting room,
shamed and stunned and silent with our rosy cheeks abloom.

A child by our side, a three inch lego up his nose,
which we both would rather leave there, but it tickles when
he blows.

I just don't get the mindset why he stores so many things
within his nasal passages – it really has to sting.

A marble from our KerPlunk game.
Two glowing ping pong balls.

An Every Flavour jellybean
found in a bathroom stall.

A peanut still inside the shell,
and though you'd hope he's through,

a solid quart of berries
that had turned his nostrils blue.

The Polly Pocket playset was a little bit too much.
Replacement parts are pricey and too hard to find and such.

I try to gently warn him while I'm biting back the sass,
if I find another thing in there, he can shove it up his ass.

Say Cheese!

The only photos that we own of
children three and four
are the ones they take at school
each year - the ones that they
abhor.

Wearing all the careworn hand-
me-downs from offspring one
and two.
No matter what the style or fit
or fabric color hue.

It isn't like they are not loved,
not any more or less.
But the newness of the
parenting had worn off we
confess.

Our firstborn has two portrait
paintings, some skywriting, and
more.
Our second many glamour shots
we took at fancy stores.

The third and fourth, they came
as one, and wallet they impact.
Amazing we could feed them
with our bank account intact.

So, admittedly, the only pics we
have of darling twins.
Are the school proofs stamped
as 'SAMPLE' and the envelopes
they're in.

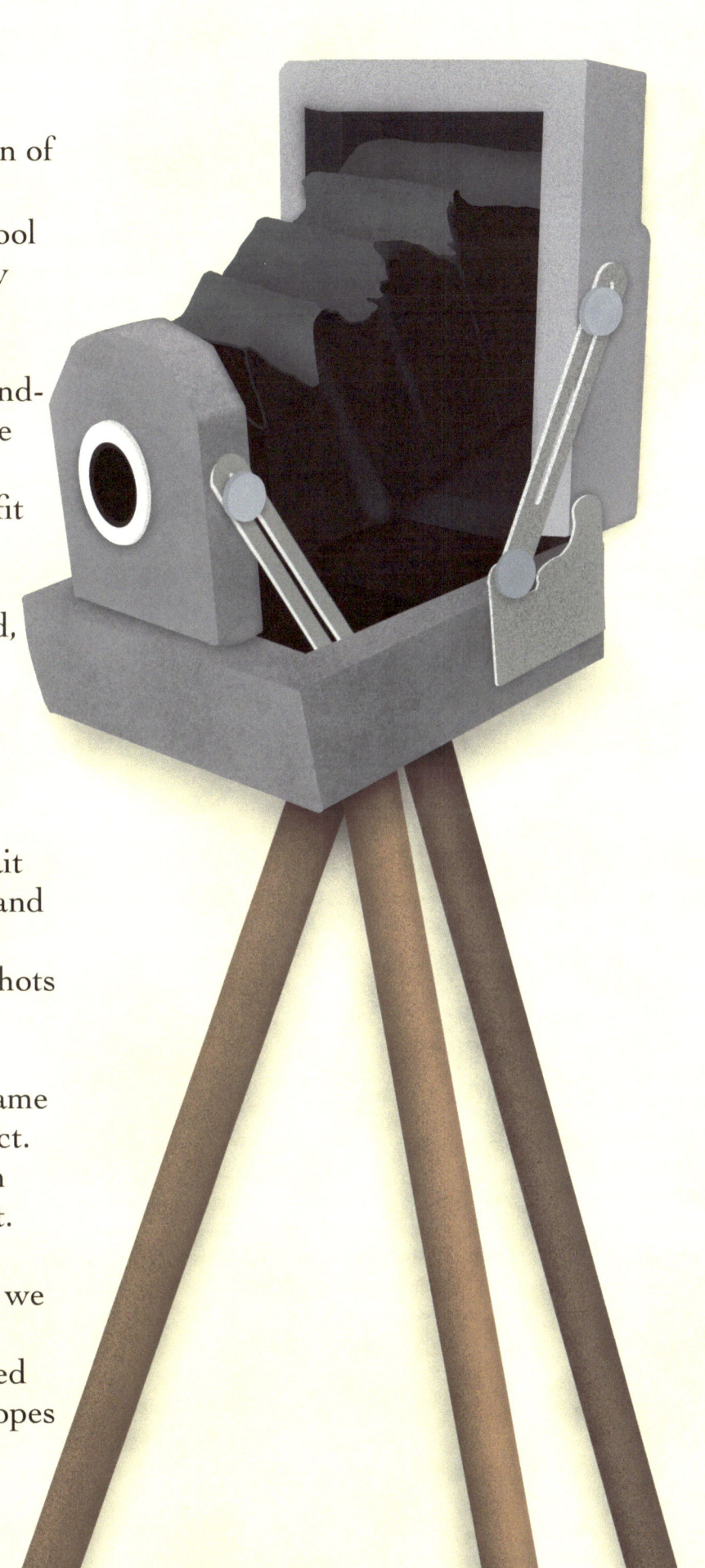

The Hoarder

My daughter was a vengeful squirrel. When angered by a fight or quarrel, she'd stew and watch and bide her time, then quietly carry out her crimes. Favorite trinkets long thought lost, as victims searched 'til eyes were crossed.

Hidden deep beneath her bed, hair clipped from her ex-boyfriends' heads.

Santa's favorite cap and vest. All five cones from her driving test.

A sliver of her teacher's soul, her breathalyzer, and dashboard troll.

My nitro pills, her mom's glass eye. Some handcuffs from her DUI.

They gathered dust and signs of age, in honor to her silent rage. A monolith beneath her bed. That land where only fools would tread.

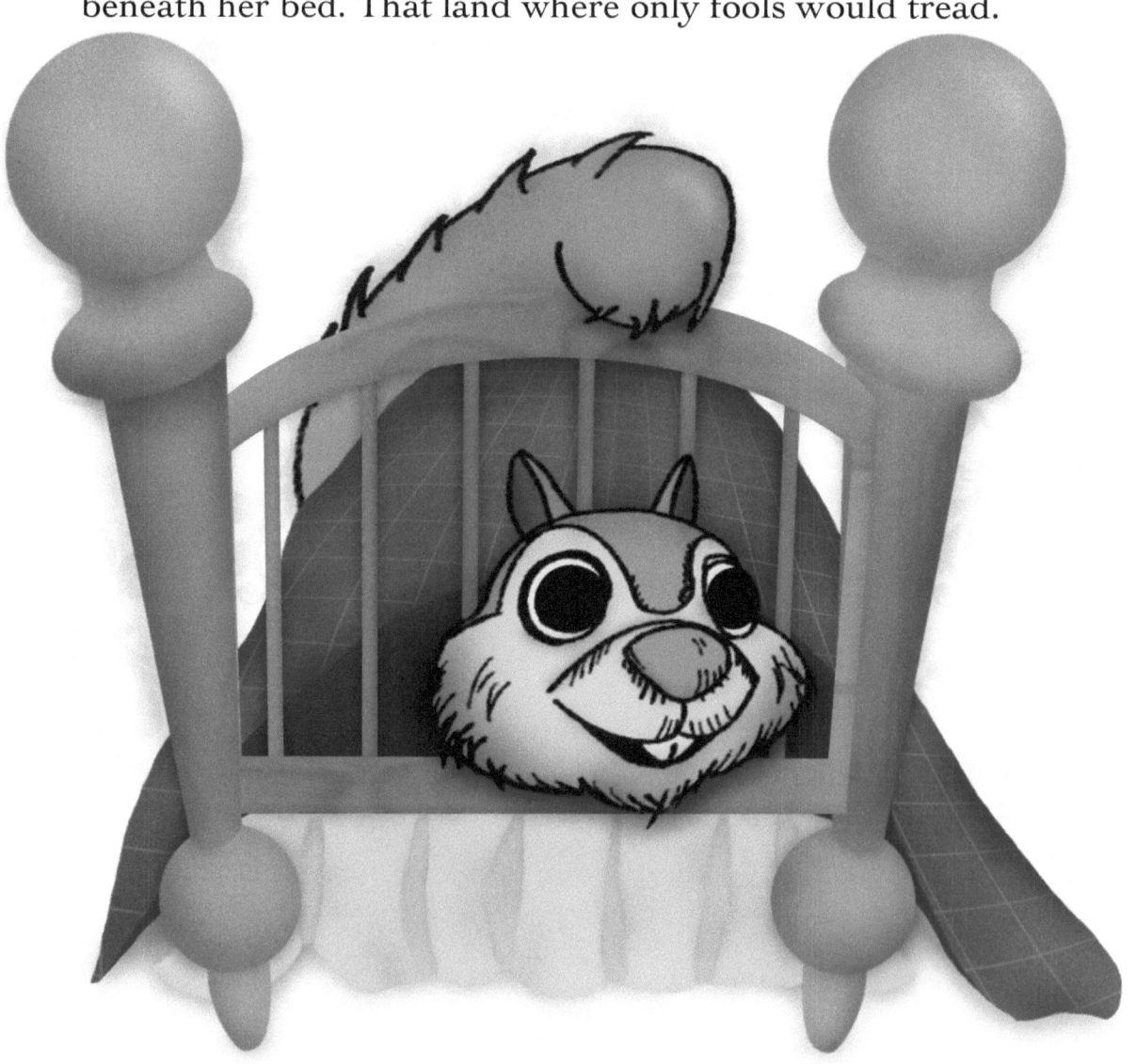

von Trapp

Midwestern von Trapps,
We just break into song.
Whether cleaning the kitchen
or mowing the lawn.

Skipping and frolicking
throughout the day.
Silly old melodies.
Nothing to say.

Sad note from the choir
about our tone deaf first child.
The other members begged us,
"Send him back to the wild!"

Tower of Terror

You see us approaching a mile away,
as our tower-shaped minivan bounces and sways.

The people that pass us don't understand why
the luggage we pack nearly scratches the sky.

With a screeching of arguing voices and cries
that escape through the gaps in the window pane eyes.

The AC is blaring, yet the windows are steamed.
A modern eighth wonder on a road trip it seems.

Dad clenches the steering with blanching white knuckles
and mom rolls her eyes while she chokes back a chuckle.

As the kids are all chanting the 45th verse
of the beers on the wall song, the same as the first.

Virus Verbosity

Snot and sneezes, poop and pee.
Seeping eyes are haunting me.

The nasty things that drip out of
a child.
All the miscreant fluids and
solids so vile.

But they've grown up and gone
and yet I am still here.
I need not have succumbed to
my germaphobe fear.

It's truly amazing I survived it
somehow,
though I think I just *may* have a
temperature now.

Dress Rehearsal

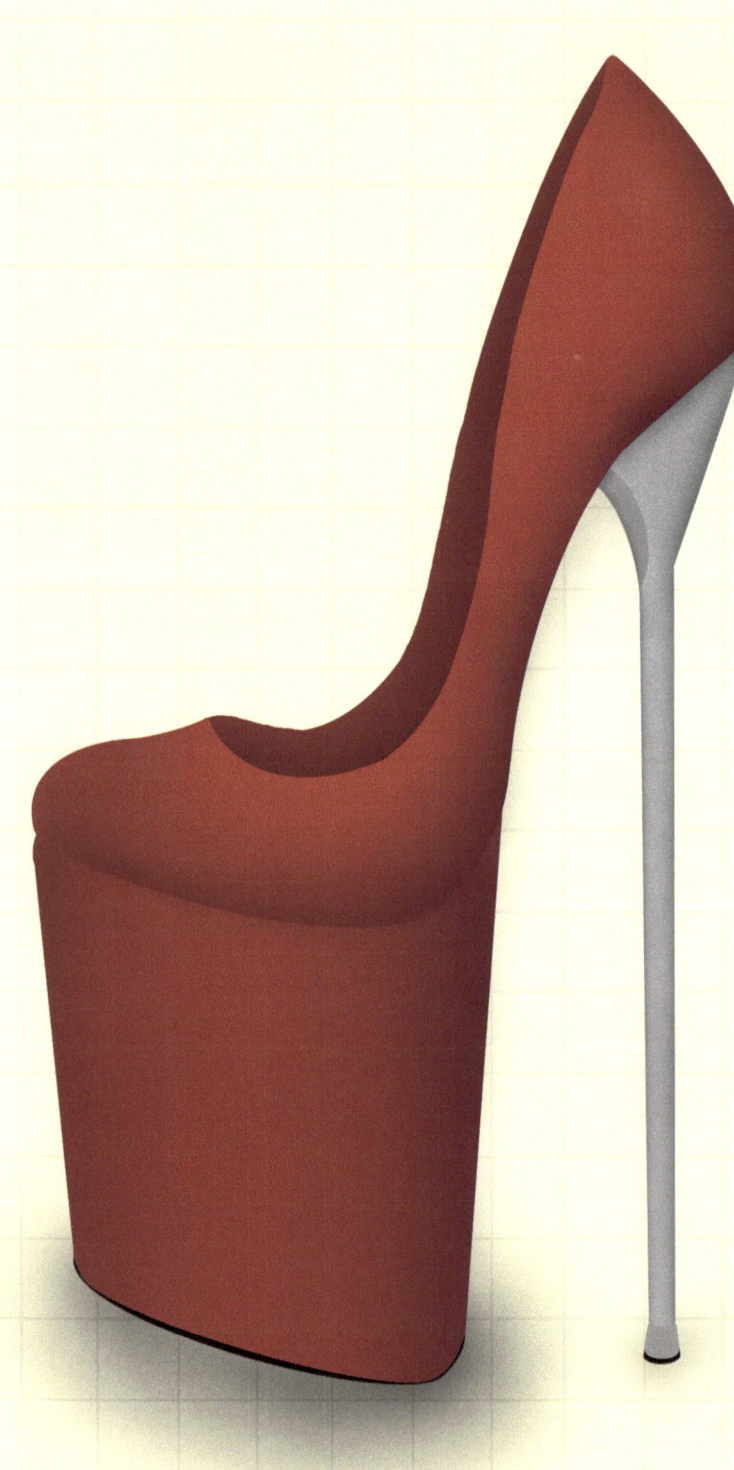

Always in rehearsal, my small child is in dress,
preparing for performances – the spotlight of success.

His director is his sister, with a goal to reach the stars,
to squeeze the kind of drama from his act to take them far.

They've stolen all the blankets just to build a makeshift stage.
Their shows are waaaay off Broadway, quite the dreamers of their age.

Four table lamps are missing, extension cords as well.
Their lighting's overheating, it's a sweaty Dante's Hell.

The BO starts your eyes to water, musty nostril funk.
In their latest show of *Bambi*, they both could have played the skunk.

The passing years were not too kind, and Broadway never called.
Our little troupe heartbroken, the cast and crew appalled.

The show has closed; my daughter claims she lost her lustful zeal.
My son still headlines drag queen shows – he loves to strut the heels.

Tug and Pull

What was I thinking, leaving mommy to sleep,
in her labor recovery, counting more sheep?

I'm here at the zoo with two kids in a cart
and the two more on tethers near tear me apart.

I'm starting to wonder as animals stare,
if they pity me passing,
our misery shared.

I then got my answer
at the elephant house.
One threw me a peanut,
and one for my spouse.

Point and Click

Three of our four children as we taught our tots to read, some learning interventions were we told that they would need.

A little more attention and a little extra love, functionally iterate when push would come to shove.

We think that our society is a little out of touch
and of this silly shortfall, it is making way too much.

It's no failure of the parents, who get slapped with feedback blunt,
as long as the three idiots can point and click and grunt.

The One

One obsessed with serial killers; one dreams of robbing banks.

One can hotwire cars and does some other techie pranks.

One is narcissistic and the center of the world.

One is starting fist fights, always strutting with fists curled.

One may think that this would get a parent down and sickly.

One benefit of shallowness – I do get past it quickly.

Tiptoe Master

Every knothole, every board.
Echoing steps and squeaks galore.
He was master of his parents' domain.
His acrobat skills put a circus to shame.

He could cross the old house with his shoes in his hands.
All while holding his breath; on his tiptoes, he'd stand.
Creeping along in the pitch of black.
Deftly moving, avoiding all cracks.

If he was caught late again; his life would be over,
'cause he lost his best jeans when he wasn't quite sober.

Carload Blues

Movie projecting, outdoor screen.
Steamed car windows and muffled screams.

Candy and popcorn and cardiacs.
Four sets of feet shoved in my back.

Why did we come here and what was I thinking?
The minivan's groaning with stifled sock stinking.

But I paid by the carload for monsters and creatures.
So I must stick it out to the end of the feature.

About the Unfortunate Author

John David Kegg was born poor and remains poor, so please send money for his care. He has needs.

In the absence of a proper photograph, the artist rendering at right should give you a vague idea of what's going on there. You may wish to avert your eyes and shield those of small children.

When not writing and illustrating silly, tongue-in-cheek bedtime stories, our friend spends his time running very slowly, kayaking even more slowly, and being tormented by his spouse and four disrespectful children. Children who were likely delivered by stork to the the wrong household because they are attractive, bright, and well-adjusted members of society.

Further author ramblings, updates about upcoming book releases or audiobook recordings of stories like *Beware the Reenie* or *Pardon Pete and the Gobbler Retreat*, and other musings may be found at www.bewarethereenie.com.

Books from John David Kegg

**Illustrated Books for Ages 8-99
(available on Amazon.com):**
"Beware the Reenie"
"Wish Upon a Haunted Star"
"How to Crack a Kringle"
"Pardon Pete and the Gobbler Retreat"

**Illustrated Books for Ages 17+:
(available on Amazon.com)**
"The Seesaw Missile Launcher and Other Parenting Fails"

**Audiobooks:
(available on Audible/Amazon/iTunes)**
"Beware the Reenie"
(available now)
" Pardon Pete and the Gobbler Retreat"
(available October 2023)
"How to Crack a Kringle"
(available November 2023)

BEWARE THE REENIE

SPOOKY FUN FOR AGES 8-99!

WRITTEN AND ILLUSTRATED BY
JOHN DAVID KEGG

"BEWARE THE REENIE" IS A SPOOKY, TONGUE-IN-CHEEK TALE FOR AGES 8 TO 99…

…A TALE OF THE DAY THE REENIE CAME TO TOWN. THE REENIE IS ANGRY, THE REENIE IS HUNGRY, AND THE REENIE IS SEARCHING FOR ITS NEXT MEAL. SO MAYBE, JUST MAYBE, YOU SHOULD WATCH YOUR STEP… BEFORE THE REENIE DECIDES TO DINE WITH YOU!

Every year before Thanksgiving, that special holiday dedicated to eating your weight in second helpings, the president dramatically pardons one lucky turkey in all the land.

That bird receives the golden turkey ticket to a secret paradise where all the pardoned turkeys live in sleepy poultry peace. No more nightmares about grocery freezer aisles, shrink wrap, and ladle after ladle of gibblet gravy. It is every turkey's dream come true.

"Pardon Pete and the Gobbler Retreat" is the tale of a local hero, Pardon Pete, the bravest turkey tom to ever gobble, who risked it all to run afoul of Thanksgiving tradition. So bite your beak and hold your breath, as Pardon Pete does a dance with death! **Disclaimer:** Naps are often needed after reading stories about turkeys.

"How to Crack a Kringle" is a jolly, tongue-in-cheek tale about the little known year Santa walked away from Christmas with a broken heart.

The dedicated and well-meaning creatures of the North Pole decided to rally together and deliver Christmas all by themselves. Much rejoicing and pats on the back followed.

In a nutshell, it could have gone better. Much, much better.

Disclaimer - Unfortunately, I cannot promise that no elves were harmed during the telling of this story. Thank goodness they had spares.